Splish! Splash!
Dolphins and Kids Having Fun in Water

Written by Karen Board
Illustrated by Sharon Swain

Stone Fence Publishing

For Jacob and Toby!

S.S.

Cover design by Sharon Swain

Published by:
Stone Fence Publishing
Burnt Hills, NY, 12027
USA

Printed in the United States of America
ISBN: 978-0-9827847-8-5

For Tim,
Ryan, Kevin,
and my parents —K.B.

Thank you Sharon and Mark
And a special thank you to Dr. Randy Wells, director of the Sarasota Dolphin Research Program, for his helpful comments and knowledge!

Main Characters

Olivia–age 10 loves

- swimming
- reading (especially books about dolphins)
- jokes and riddles

Jack–age 8 loves

- swimming
- collecting rocks
- drawing pictures

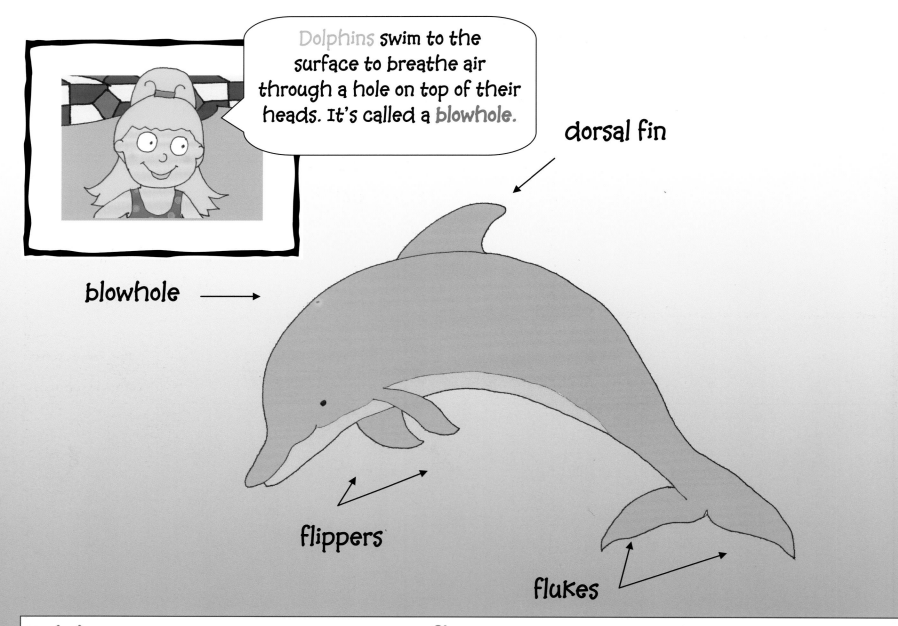

Dolphins swim to the surface to breathe air through a hole on top of their heads. It's called a blowhole.

dorsal fin

blowhole

flippers

flukes

Dolphins swim by moving their tail (**flukes**) up and down. They use their two **flippers** to control the directions they swim. The **dorsal fin** helps keep dolphins balanced.

I wonder what other ways I'm like a dolphin.

Dolphins are mammals, just like us. Dogs and cats are mammals too. Like all mammals:

- Dolphins breathe air into their lungs.
- Dolphins are warm-blooded. This means their body temperature is controlled by their bodies, not the outside temperature.
- Baby dolphins (calves) are fed with milk from their mother's body.

Dolphins are among the smartest of all animals.

Are there any other mammals that live in the water?

Mammals living in the sea can be divided into three groups.

Sharks are not mammals—they are fish

1. Whales, dolphins, porpoises (same structure, different sizes)
2. Seals, sea otters, walruses, polar bears, and sea lions (live on land and in the water)
3. Dugongs (live mostly in seawater)
and manatees (live both in freshwater and seawater)

Knock, Knock

Who's there? Whale

Whale who?

WHALE you show me some pictures of marine mammals?

polar bear

sea lion

manatee

porpoise

walrus

whale

dolphin

dugong

seal

sea otter

90 feet

- Blue whales are the largest mammal ever to live on Earth. They can grow to a length of 100 feet and weigh as much as 160 tons!
- Porpoises are the smallest members of the whale family. Porpoises have shorter beaks and flatter teeth than dolphins.

The fastest humans can swim in short bursts at around 4.5 mph. If a dolphin was in the Olympics, he would get the gold!

Ways Dolphins Like to Play: SPLASH! Spin, jump, leap, and dive. Some dolphins surf the tops of waves!

Some kids like to jump or dive off a diving board.

How to dive:

- Standing up or kneeling at the side of a pool, keep your chin tucked in and put your arms over your head.
- Bend over and push yourself off the side of the pool.
- Have your hands enter the water first and your feet enter the water last.

> SAFETY TIP-NEVER DIVE INTO SHALLOW WATER! NEVER DIVE WHEN YOU DON'T KNOW WHAT IS UNDERWATER!

Some kids like to play a game called Marco Polo.

How to play Marco Polo:

Get a group of kids. Choose one person to be Marco Polo. This player closes her eyes and counts to 10 while the other players scatter in the pool. After the count, Marco swims around with her eyes closed trying to tag another player. To help find the other players, Marco Polo calls out "Marco!" and the other players call out "Polo!" Once she tags another player, that player becomes Marco.

Some kids like to race when they swim. Some kids join a swim team.

Kids on a swim team learn four strokes: freestyle, backstroke, breaststroke, and butterfly.

breaststroke

In the breaststroke, the swimmer floats on his or her stomach, with the legs bent a little. The swimmer's arms begin outstretched, with the hands almost touching, and push outward from each other in a circular motion. Arms may not come out of the water. At the same time, the knees are brought forward toward the chest and then kicked outward like a frog. During a cycle of one arm and one leg kick, the swimmer's head breaks the surface of the water for a breath.

butterfly

To begin the butterfly, the swimmer lays facedown with arms straight ahead. The swimmer pulls the arms outward, then deeper into the water, and then back toward his or her legs. At the end of the stroke, the swimmer's arms come out of the water and are thrown forward to the starting position. As the arms come out of the water, the swimmer lifts his or her head for a breath. The DOLPHIN KICK is used for the butterfly.

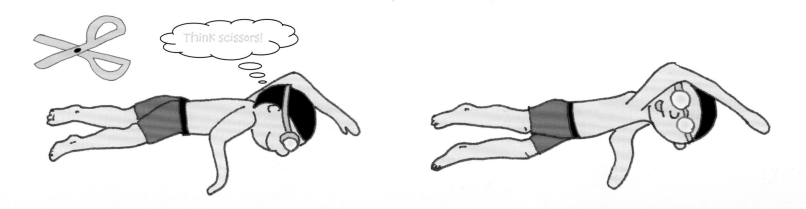

freestyle

Freestyle swimmers, facedown in the water, move their arms overhead one at a time. To breathe, they turn their head to the side every few strokes. Freestyle swimmers use a flutter kick, moving their legs up and down like scissors.

backstroke

The backstroke is an upside-down version of freestyle. On their backs in the water, backstrokers lift their arms overhead one at a time and pull themselves along. They also use a flutter kick, and they can take a breath whenever they need to because their faces are out of the water.

Most **dolphins** do not swim in a pod (a group that does not change) like many people think. They live in groups that change.

Did you know that every dolphin has a one-of-a-kind whistle! If a baby dolphin swims away, its mother gives her special whistle. The baby dolphin whistles back and swims to her mom.

Where can I find dolphins?

Splash!

Aquariums have saltwater tanks to let you watch dolphins swimming and playing underwater. There may be a special pool where trainers teach the dolphins tricks. Dolphins show off their tricks at a dolphin show! They love to leap high out of the water and make a big SPLASH! Some dolphins like to spin in the air, play with balls and Frisbees, and catch rings. Some dolphins like a tummy rub.

You can sometimes spot wild dolphins in the ocean. Dolphins live in all of the oceans in the world! Some dolphins even live in rivers.

Splish!

What would a dolphin fairy godmother give Cinderella?

Glass FLIPPERS!